SHINE ON

DOREEN CAVEN

SHINE ON

EMPOWERING AFFIRMATIONS
FOR
EXTRAORDINARY WOMEN

ILLUSTRATIONS BY YORDANKA POLEGANOVA

ROCKRIDGE
PRESS

For general information on our other products and services or to obtain technical support, please contact our Customer Care Department within the United States at (866) 744-2665, or outside the United States at (510) 253-0500.

Rockridge Press publishes its books in a variety of electronic and print formats. Some content that appears in print may not be available in electronic books, and vice versa.

TRADEMARKS: Rockridge Press and the Rockridge Press logo are trademarks or registered trademarks of Callisto Media Inc. and/or its affiliates, in the United States and other countries, and may not be used without written permission. All other trademarks are the property of their respective owners. Rockridge Press is not associated with any product or vendor mentioned in this book.

Interior and Cover Designer: Rachel Haeseker
Art Producer: Megan Baggott
Editor: Crystal Nero
Production Editor: Mia Moran

Illustration © 2020 Yordanka Poleganova
Author photo courtesy of Joan Caven

ISBN: Print 978-1-64611-547-1
eBook 978-1-64611-548-8

R0

I DEDICATE THIS BOOK TO MY
BELOVED NIECES AND NEPHEWS,
I HOPE SO MUCH FOR YOU TO
GROW UP IN A WORLD THAT
RESPECTS AND VALUES WOMEN,
NOT JUST FOR OUR SERVICE
TO OTHERS, BUT FOR WHO
WE ARE AS UNIQUE PEOPLE.

CONTENTS

✦

"THE WHOLE POINT OF
BEING ALIVE IS TO EVOLVE
INTO THE COMPLETE PERSON
YOU WERE INTENDED TO BE."

OPRAH WINFREY,
Media executive, actor, and philanthropist

INTRODUCTION

There is so much power in realizing that you are not alone.

For a long time I held in thoughts that I was hesitant to voice for fear of standing out. I was afraid that speaking honestly about my beliefs would be too disruptive to everyone around me. I prioritized the comfort of others over myself.

I continued in this silence until I could no longer justify staying quiet about the real issues that affected my life. I could no longer wait for change to come while doing nothing. I also realized how many other women like me had become content in discontent. Somehow, we had made a home out of being silent. In our silent solidarity, our honesty became even more of a herculean task.

How would our lives as women ever improve if we chose to remain silent about the daily problems we faced?

It was this question that spurred me to try something different. If I could be brave enough to be openly vulnerable and honest, perhaps it would encourage the next woman to know she is not alone. I wanted to create solidarity by being vocal and rejecting silence. This choice led me to a powerful awakening.

Since gifting myself with the permission to fully embrace my authenticity, my life changed immeasurably. Walking in my truth unapologetically not only led me to discover and redefine myself according to my own standards, it also introduced me to a tribe of women doing the same.

There is so much beauty in discovering who we are. The stories, wisdom, and inspiring choices shared by fellow women from all walks of life can help light our path. This discovery only comes from learning who we are outside of our fear. When we decide to speak honestly about our experiences as women and live in our authenticity, we not only release ourselves, we unlock in others the strength to do the same.

Every chapter of this book has carefully crafted affirmations to reorient your mind and inspire a motivated outlook on your life. Use it to begin your journey of living in your truth. It is my hope that you keep this book by your bedside and read an affirmation to yourself daily. Make it your morning routine to practice affirming yourself, selecting what you need from each chapter to guide you through the doubts, insecurities, and concerns that plague your life.

Changing how you think is the most powerful step in transforming your life. I encourage you to be consistent and try to apply action to each affirmation. With time, these positive thoughts will feel like home to you and set you on your own journey to rule the world.

You'll also find some of my favorite quotes from fierce and inspiring women around the world. They will help you envision yourself as capable of being just as powerful and fierce as the women who uttered them.

It is my belief that the greatest gift we can give ourselves is to live our lives as honestly as we can. Learning to see the value in our true selves gives us the strength to demand what we deserve and adamantly reject what we don't.

You are powerful; you just have to believe it. Isn't it amazing what we can achieve once we learn to see ourselves as deserving?

CHAPTER 1

MIND, BODY & SPIRIT

♦

"IT'S WHEN THE DISCOMFORT
STRIKES THAT THEY REALIZE A
STRONG MIND IS THE MOST
POWERFUL WEAPON OF ALL."

CHRISSIE WELLINGTON,
Triathlete and four-time Ironman Triathlon World Champion

FIERCE FIRST

JANET GUTHRIE

JANET GUTHRIE's love for adventure started early. She earned a pilot's license at the age of 17 and decided to pursue a career in the aerospace industry. After graduating with a degree in physics from the University of Michigan in 1960, she started a career in aviation.

Janet's passion for adventure led her to apply for NASA's scientist-astronaut program. Although she was eliminated after the first round of interviews, Janet was undeterred by this closed door and turned to car racing instead.

At a time when women were considered to be too fragile to participate in motorsports, Janet built her own engine, did her own body work, and was a skilled driver. She made a name for herself in the Sports Car Club of America circuit and began competing in major races. Despite her successes, she faced criticism from the public and press, who questioned her ability to perform on the racetrack. She didn't let that stop her.

While she didn't qualify for the Indianapolis 500 in 1976, Janet tried again in 1977 and became the first woman to compete not only in the Indianapolis 500 but also in the Daytona 500. Mechanical issues at the Indy 500 racetrack caused her to finish in 29th place in 1977, but she returned in 1978 and came in ninth—in spite of competing with a broken wrist! Because of the sexism she faced, Janet struggled to find sponsor-ships, which was one of her biggest challenges as a race car driver. She was still able to compete professionally with a budget that was a small fraction of the amount being spent by the top teams—all helmed by men.

Janet's relentless pursuit of her dreams led the way for future race car drivers like Simona de Silvestro, Ana Beatriz, and Danica Patrick. Her perseverance, skill, and bravery changed history as we know it!

"I was the key figure that women were pointing to and saying, 'Look, she can do this; I can do this.' It was a role that I did not seek but came to recognize as a responsibility."

—JANET GUTHRIE

I AM CAPABLE OF ACHIEVING
GREATNESS BEYOND MY
PRESENT IMAGINATION.

▲

MY DOUBTS ARE NO LONGER
MY MOST TRUSTED VOICE.

I AM MY BIGGEST SUPPORTER, AND I AM WORTH THE HYPE.

I AM GRATEFUL TO SEE MYSELF
AS I TRULY AM. DOUBTS AND
INSECURITIES CAN'T DISTORT
MY SELF-IMAGE.

▲

I AM DESERVING OF THE
STANDARDS I SET FOR MY
LIFE. IF IT IS NOT UP TO PAR,
I WON'T MAKE EXCUSES TO
ACCOMMODATE IT.

I AM CAREFUL AND GENTLE IN THE WAY I SPEAK TO MYSELF.

I CONTROL MY THOUGHTS,
BELIEFS, AND DESIRES.
IT IS UP TO ME TO CREATE
MY OWN NARRATIVE.

▲

LOVING MYSELF IS
NOT BEING SELFISH;
IT'S WHAT I MUST DO TO
UNDERSTAND MY VALUE.

WHEN I LOOK AT MYSELF, I CAN SEE THAT I AM STRONG, POWERFUL, HUMAN, AND VULNERABLE.

I CAN TRAIN MYSELF TO REDIRECT NEGATIVE THOUGHTS WHEN THEY APPEAR.

FIERCE FACT

SIMONE BILES is an American athlete who broke the world record for most medals won at the World Artistic Gymnastics Championships. Her total medal tally for that competition? Twenty-five, including 19 gold medals. She also made history in 2019 by being the first gymnast to perform a double-double dismount on beam at a competition and the first woman to perform a triple-double in a gymnastics competition. Even though she could have faced career repercussions, Simone spoke out against the USA Gymnastics establishment that allowed a sexual predator to target her and other gymnasts over multiple decades. For her bravery, she and more than 300 other sexual assault survivors won the Arthur Ashe Courage Award at the 2018 ESPY Awards.

I RESPECT THE COMPLEXITY
OF MY BODY. I WILL NOT TAKE
MY BODY FOR GRANTED.

▲

I JUDGE MY BODY BY MY OWN
STANDARDS, AND I REFUSE
TO HOLD IT TO ONE SINGULAR
DEFINITION OF BEAUTY.

I LIKE WHAT I SEE IN THE MIRROR!

I EMBRACE THE UNIQUENESS
OF MYSELF. IN SUCH A
DIVERSE WORLD, I GET TO
LOOK LIKE ME.

▲

I AM TOO VALUABLE TO TREAT
MY BODY WITH DISREGARD.

MY BODY DOES SO MANY AMAZING THINGS, AND IT DESERVES THE BEST CARE AND THE HIGHEST PRAISE.

MY BODY IS STRONG AND CAPABLE OF HEALING.

EVERY CELL IN MY BODY IS
DESERVING OF LOVE, LIGHT,
AND TENDERNESS.

▲

MY BODY IS MY ONLY HOME,
AND I FEEL STRONG AND
BLESSED TO INHABIT IT.

I LOVE MY BODY FULLY WITH NO BUTS, IFS, OR MAYBES.

FIERCE FACT

SAROJINI NAIDU was a women's rights activist and poet born in Hyderabad, India, in 1879. She was active in the movement for women's suffrage and lectured on women's rights, social welfare, and Indian nationalism. Sarojini fought for India's emancipation from colonial rule and was incarcerated multiple times for her political activities. In 1925, she was elected the first female president of the Indian National Congress Party. After India's independence from Britain in 1947, she became the governor of Uttar Pradesh, making her the nation's first female governor. She died in 1949, still in office.

MY PRESENCE IS A GIFT.

▲

I SOAR ABOVE THE DOUBTS AND INSECURITIES THAT MAKE ME QUESTION MY WORTHINESS.

I AM CONFIDENT IN THE BEAUTY MY SOUL EMITS.

I AM UNIQUE IN EVERY WAY
AND PROUD OF WHAT MAKES
ME DIFFERENT.

I NOURISH MY SOUL
WITH THE LOVE I HAVE
FOR MYSELF AND FOR OTHERS.

I RADIATE LOVE, LIGHT, AND POSITIVITY.

I AM INSPIRED BY THE DIFFERENCES THAT MAKE US ALL UNIQUE.

I AM UNTAMABLE. MY
SOUL CANNOT BE OWNED,
RESTRAINED, OR CONTROLLED.

▲

I ACHIEVE SO MUCH
BY EMBRACING THE FIRE
INSIDE MY SOUL.

MY AUTHENTICITY IS POTENT,
AND MY VOICE ECHOES THE
CRIES OF MY SPIRIT.

MY WORLD GLOWS
BRIGHTLY BECAUSE OF MY
PRESENCE IN IT.

I AM THE SOURCE OF LIGHT ON MY OWN PATH.

MY BODY IS NOT A HOST
FOR NEGATIVE THOUGHTS
TO MAKE A HOME. MY BODY
IS A PLACE WHERE MY
SOUL WHISPERS WORDS OF
ENCOURAGEMENT TO ME.

▲

I AM ENRICHED BY THE POWER
MY SOUL EMITS AND THE
PURPOSE IT GIVES ME.

I HAVE ALWAYS BEEN ENOUGH.

FIERCE FACT

ELIZABETH WANAMAKER PERATROVICH was a Tlingit native born in Petersburg, Alaska, in 1911. Although she experienced segregation growing up, she was shocked to see the blatant discrimination of the indigenous community when she returned to Petersburg after living in Bellingham, Washington, for a decade. Elizabeth, along with her husband Roy Peratrovich, decided to do something to improve the plight of their people.

Together, they lobbied for an anti-discrimination bill, campaigned for Alaska Natives to gain seats in the legislature, and traveled across the state to gain more support for their cause. Their work resulted in the passage of the Anti-Discrimination Act of 1945, the first law of its kind in the United States.

Today, February 16 is recognized in Alaska as Elizabeth Peratrovich Day in recognition of her courage and efforts to bring dignity to the lives of Alaska Natives.

◆

"I HAVE TO CONSTANTLY
RE-IDENTIFY MYSELF TO MYSELF,
REACTIVATE MY OWN STANDARDS,
MY OWN CONVICTIONS ABOUT
WHAT I'M DOING AND WHY."

NINA SIMONE,
Singer, songwriter, musician, and civil rights activist

CHAPTER 2

LOVE, LIFE & EVERYTHING NICE

✦

"A THING EMERGED, WHICH
WAS MY ACTUAL PERSONALITY
AND MY ACTUAL VOICE . . .
AND I REALIZED THAT I WAS
FUNNY AND ALLOWED TO BE—
AND ALLOWED TO BE LOUD,
AND OBNOXIOUS—AND I TOOK
FULL ADVANTAGE OF IT."

MERYL STREEP,
Actor and women's rights activist

FIERCE FIRST

MALALA YOUSAFZAI

MALALA YOUSAFZAI was raised in the Swat Valley in Pakistan. She attended a girls' school founded by her father, an educator who championed women getting an education. Malala was 11 years old when the Taliban took control of the area in 2007, barring girls from attending school. Although she was unable to pursue her education, her voice would not be silenced.

Less than a year after she was forced to leave school, she gave a speech at a press club in Peshawar, Pakistan. "How dare the Taliban take away my basic right to education," she said. Her speech quickly circulated throughout Pakistan, and she was soon approached to blog for BBC about her experience living under the Taliban rule. To be safe, she began blogging under a different name, "Gul Makai," and wrote entries about her daily life.

As her platform grew, she went public. Her activism for girls' educations garnered her television appearances and international media coverage. On October 9, 2012, a gunman boarded a bus she was riding with her friends, asked, "Who is Malala?" then shot the 15-year-old girl in the head. She survived the attack, but her injuries were serious, and she was flown to Birmingham, England, where she underwent multiple surgeries.

Her attack shocked the world, and massive support poured in from millions of people. After her recovery, Malala became a worldwide symbol for peace.

In 2014, Malala was awarded the Nobel Peace Prize, alongside Indian children's rights activist Kailash Satyarthi. At the age of 17, Malala became the youngest Nobel laureate ever.

Malala's activism continues through the Malala Fund, which she established in 2013 to help girls access free, quality education in their home countries. She had the bravery to speak up for her right to live the life she wanted—not just for herself but for girls all over the world.

"Though I appear as one girl, one person, who is five foot two inches tall . . . I am not a lone voice, I am many."

—MALALA YOUSAFZAI

I EXUDE THE LOVE I HAVE
FOR MYSELF AND THE LOVE
I HAVE FOR OTHERS.

I AM WORTHY OF LOVE
THAT IS RESPECTFUL.
I EMBRACE LOVE THAT IS
HEALTHY AND NURTURING.

I DESERVE THE TYPE OF LOVE I AM WILLING TO GIVE.

LOVING MYSELF TEACHES ME
HOW I WANT TO BE LOVED.

I FORGIVE MYSELF FOR THE
TIMES I DIDN'T LOVE ME
ENOUGH.

I AM WORTHY OF LOVE THAT CELEBRATES MY AUTHENTICITY AND IS NOT THREATENED BY MY RADIANCE.

I DELIGHT IN THE
KNOWLEDGE THAT I AM
MY FIRST CHOICE, ALWAYS.

I AM OPEN TO LOVE
THAT DEEPENS THE
LOVE I HAVE FOR MYSELF.

I AM GRATEFUL TO BE SURROUNDED BY LOVE THAT ENCOURAGES MY FREEDOM.

I DESERVE TRANSFORMATIVE LOVE THAT BRINGS OUT THE BEST OF ME.

FIERCE FACT

DOLORES HUERTA is an American Latina activist and labor leader who founded the United Farm Workers with Cesar Chavez in 1962. She organized farmworkers so they could collectively fight for their rights. In 1965, she led a strike of 5,000 California grape workers demanding better working conditions. She helped negotiate contracts, establish health care and unemployment benefits, and reduce workers' exposure to harmful pesticides. Dolores was instrumental in pushing for the 1975 Agricultural Labor Relations Act, a pioneer law that recognized the rights of California farmworkers to bargain for better wages and conditions. In 2000, she started campaigning for more Latinas to run for political office.

Dolores remains a feminist activist fighting for equality.

I AM HONORED TO BE THE
CARETAKER OF MY LIFE.

I AM OPEN TO THE LESSONS
I LEARN IN MY LIFE JOURNEY.

MY LIFE IS A GIFT, AND USING MY TALENTS IS HOW I SHOW MY GRATITUDE.

I ATTRACT POSITIVITY, LOVE,
AND KINDNESS INTO MY LIFE.

I DO NOT DISRESPECT MY LIFE
BY WANTING SOMEONE ELSE'S.

MY LIFE IS WORTH THE EFFORT AND CARE I PUT INTO IT.

I AM WORTHY
OF MY OWN LOVE.

I AM PATIENT, RESPECTFUL,
AND ENCOURAGING OF MY
LIFE BECAUSE IT DESERVES
MY KINDNESS.

LIVING MY LIFE AUTHENTICALLY IS LOVING MYSELF IN THE DEEPEST SENSE.

I AM IN CONTROL OF WHAT
I ALLOW IN MY LIFE.

MY HAPPINESS IS CENTERED
IN MY FREEDOM TO LIVE
THE LIFE THAT I WANT.

DELAYS IN MY LIFE ARE HOW I LEARN PATIENCE. I APPRECIATE THE PERIODS OF TRANSITION IN MY LIFE.

FAILURES IN MY LIFE ARE
HOW I LEARN PERSISTENCE. I
APPRECIATE THE GRIT I LEARN
FROM CHALLENGING MYSELF.

DESPITE IT ALL, I AM AT PEACE
WITH MY LIFE.

WHEN IT COMES TO MY LIFE, OTHERS CAN LEAVE THEIR NEGATIVE INPUT AT THE DOOR BEFORE THEY WALK IN.

＊

FIERCE FACT

FLORA NWAPA is known as the mother of modern African literature. Her first book, *Efuru*, was released in 1966, making her one of the first the first female authors to be published in Nigeria. Although the literary community was heavily male-dominated, Flora was not content to let her female characters fall into traditionally expected roles, and her novels depicted Nigerian culture from a woman's perspective.

When Flora became unsatisfied with the way her publishers were promoting her books, she cut ties with them and founded Tana Press, Ltd., becoming her own publisher. She founded a second publishing house and named it after herself: the Flora Nwapa Company. She promoted not only her own writing but also the work of other women writers.

✦

"THOSE PARTS OF YOURSELF THAT
YOU DESPERATELY WANT TO HIDE
AND DESTROY WILL GAIN POWER
OVER YOU. THE BEST THING TO
DO IS FACE AND OWN THEM,
BECAUSE THEY ARE FOREVER A
PART OF YOU."

JANET MOCK,

Writer, director, and transgender rights activist

CHAPTER 3

WORK IT!

✦

"I AM NOT LUCKY. YOU KNOW
WHAT I AM? I AM SMART, I AM
TALENTED, I TAKE ADVANTAGE OF
THE OPPORTUNITIES THAT COME
MY WAY AND I WORK REALLY,
REALLY HARD. DON'T CALL ME
LUCKY. CALL ME A *BADASS*."

SHONDA RHIMES,
Television producer, writer, and director

FIERCE FIRST

SHIRLEY CHISHOLM

SHIRLEY CHISHOLM was born in Brooklyn, New York. The oldest of four daughters, she went to public schools in Brooklyn and then attended Brooklyn College, graduating in 1946 with honors. Her professors encouraged her to pursue a political career, but she was wary, citing that she bore a "double handicap," being both black and a woman. She worked as a nursery school teacher, and in 1951, she earned her master's degree in early childhood education from Columbia University.

By 1960, she was working as a consultant in the Division of Day Care in New York's Office of Children and Family Services. Passionate about social justice, Shirley joined local chapters of the National Association for the Advancement of Colored People, the League of Women Voters, and the Democratic party club in Bedford-Stuyvesant, Brooklyn.

Her own political career took off in 1964 when she was voted into the New York State Legislature, the second black person elected. Shirley pushed through a program that provides financial support and counseling to low-income students enrolled in local colleges to this day.

In 1968, Shirley became the first black woman elected to the House of Representatives. She dedicated her time in Congress to enacting changes that addressed racial, gender, and economic inequalities. Shirley was a founding member of the Congressional Black Caucus. She fought for unemployment benefits for domestic workers and sponsored a bill to ensure that they received minimum wage. She fought for the Equal Rights Amendment, which would have guaranteed equal protection under the law to women. She fought for women's reproductive freedom, school lunch programs, and publicly funded day care. She protested the massive spending on the Vietnam War.

Despite her substantial achievements, her decision to run for the presidency in 1972 was treated as a spectacle rather than with the respect her candidacy deserved. She was blocked from participating in the televised primary debates and had to take legal action to be allowed to make just one speech. Shirley Chisholm lost the election, but her will to fight to get her voice heard, even while knowing the odds were against her, is an inspiration to all women to be just as courageous. Her fearless spirit was right up front in her campaign slogan: "unbought and unbossed."

"I want history to remember me... not as the first black woman to have made a bid for the presidency of the United States, but as a black woman who lived in the 20th century and who dared to be herself. I want to be remembered as a catalyst for change in America."

—SHIRLEY CHISHOLM

I WILL ACCOMPLISH THE
GOALS I HAVE SET.

A CLOSED DOOR IS NOT THE
END OF MY DREAMS; IT IS THE
OPENING TO NEW DREAMS.

MY AUTHENTICITY ADDS TO MY SUCCESS.

I HAVE NO ROOM TO DOUBT MY
ABILITIES. MY SKILLS TAKE UP
ALL THE SPACE.

THE OPPORTUNITIES
THAT ARE PERFECT FOR
ME WILL FIND ME.

I WILL KEEP PUTTING IN EFFORT BECAUSE I DESERVE SUCCESS.

I AM ABUNDANTLY SKILLED.
I CAN DO IT, SO I WILL.

I WILL DEMAND WHAT
I REQUIRE BECAUSE
I AM WORTH IT.

BAD DAYS ARE NEEDED REST DAYS AND NOT PROOF THAT I CAN'T CUT IT.

I AM FOCUSED ON MYSELF; I HAVE NO TIME OR DESIRE TO COMPETE WITH OTHER PEOPLE.

FIERCE FACT

VERA RUBIN was an American astrophysicist who upended modern physics and astronomy with her groundbreaking research that confirmed the existence of dark matter. She faced obstacles as a woman in science even as a young girl and recalled later in life, "My science teacher once told me I wasn't good enough for science and look at me now." Vera earned her bachelor's degree in 1948, and after Princeton University's PhD program rejected her because of her gender, she earned her doctorate from Georgetown University. During her early career, much of her work was rejected by her colleagues and considered immensely controversial. Today, Rubin's work is considered pivotal to our understanding of the cosmos.

I AM PROUD OF MY
ACCOMPLISHMENTS AND
CELEBRATE MY GIFTS.

MY CONTRIBUTIONS ARE
IMPORTANT AND NECESSARY.

I ENJOY MY SUCCESS, AND I WILL NOT APOLOGIZE FOR IT.

NO MATTER HOW SUCCESSFUL
I AM, I WILL ALWAYS PUSH
MYSELF TO KEEP LEARNING.

MY POTENTIAL EXCEEDS
MY WILDEST DREAMS.

FAILURE OCCURS ON
THE ROAD TO SUCCESS.
I AM PREPARED FOR IT.

MISTAKES CONTAIN
LESSONS, AND LESSONS
SPROUT GROWTH.

MY AGE ALONE IS NOT AN
EXCUSE FOR ME TO GIVE UP.

THE JOURNEY WILL HAVE
HIGHS AND LOWS, BUT MY
TENACITY WILL BE CONSTANT.

I HAVE NO DOUBT THAT I WILL GET TO MY DESTINATION. IT'S WHAT I WAS CREATED TO DO.

FIERCE FACT

In 1964, PATSY TAKEMOTO MINK ran a grassroots campaign for Hawaii's second seat in the House of Representatives, without the support of the Democratic establishment, and won. The Japanese American attorney became the first woman of color to be elected to the US House of Representatives. While serving as a congresswoman, Patsy fought for gender and racial equality, bilingual education, and universal health care. She was almost able to establish a national day care system, but it was vetoed by President Richard Nixon in 1971. In the 1970s, she spoke out against the Vietnam War. She was a driving force behind the passage of Title IX in 1972. This law, co-authored and sponsored by Patsy, is an important civil rights law that says any educational institution that receives federal funding cannot deny opportunities to students on the basis of gender. Her contribution resulted in remarkable growth in women's collegiate athletics programs. After she died in 2002, Title IX was renamed the Patsy T. Mink Equal Opportunity in Education Act.

✦

"I'M TOUGH, I'M AMBITIOUS,
AND I KNOW EXACTLY
WHAT I WANT. IF THAT
MAKES ME A B*TCH, OKAY."

MADONNA,
Singer, songwriter, and actor

◆

CHAPTER 4

YOUR TRIBE

◆

"AS WOMEN, WE HAVE TO
STOP BEING SCARED TO BE
THE WOMEN WE WANT TO BE,
AND WE HAVE TO RAISE
OUR DAUGHTERS TO BE THE
WOMEN THEY WANT TO BE—
NOT THE WOMEN WE THINK
THEY SHOULD BE."

JADA PINKETT SMITH,
Actor, screenwriter, singer-songwriter, and producer

FIERCE FIRST

WANGARI MAATHAI

WANGARI MAATHAI was born in a rural area of Kenya in 1940. After obtaining her PhD, she became a professor of veterinary anatomy, and while she was teaching, she joined Kenya's National Council of Women.

In 1976, Wangari wanted to address the complaints of rural Kenyan women whose lives were negatively affected by environmental degradation and food insecurity. Wangari believed in the power of teamwork and community-based solutions. She decided to pursue community-based tree planting. Wangari thought that once the women in a given community began improving the sustainability of their community, everyone else would take notice and follow suit. She founded the Green Belt Movement as a grassroots organization focused on reducing poverty and conserving the environment.

Wangari soon realized that for conservation to be successful, her work needed to address the root of the degradation, which was the government's mishandling of natural resources. Many of Kenya's forests were being cleared and replaced with commercial plantations that relied on low-wage labor, causing both environmental destruction and poverty. The Green Belt Movement began advocating for greater political accountability. This meant that Wangari was criticizing the Kenyan government, putting her safety in jeopardy. In 1992, she was arrested for sedition and treason for daring to speak out in favor of democracy and conservation. She was beaten by police for protesting for the release of political prisoners. For years, she feared she would be assassinated.

But she persisted, and she later wrote in her memoir, "Every person who has ever achieved anything has been knocked down many times. But all of them picked themselves up and kept going, and that is what I have always tried to do." In 2002, she was elected into Kenya's parliament. Shortly after, she was appointed as the assistant minister of environment, natural resources, and wildlife.

In 2004, Wangari Maathai won the Nobel Peace Prize for her work to advance sustainable development, making her the first African woman to win the award. In November 2006, Wangari Maathai and five other female winners of the Nobel Peace Prize created the Nobel Women's Initiative to amplify, promote, and support women's groups around the world campaigning for justice, equality, and peace.

Since the 1970s, the Green Belt Movement has planted more than 51 million trees in Kenya.

"You cannot enslave a mind that knows itself. That values itself. That understands itself."

—WANGARI MAATHAI

I WILL BE MY AUTHENTIC SELF
WITH MY FAMILY, AND THEY
WILL LOVE THE REAL ME.

◆

I AM NOT SCARED TO TELL
MY FAMILY MEMBERS
WHEN THEY OFFEND
ME. COMMUNICATION
WILL STRENGTHEN OUR
RELATIONSHIPS.

I AM BRAVE ENOUGH TO DISAGREE WITH MEMBERS OF MY FAMILY WHEN THEIR BELIEFS ARE HARMFUL TO ME.

I AM GRATEFUL FOR
THE FAMILY THAT I HAVE
AND FOR THE LOVE THEY
BESTOW UPON ME.

◆

I WILL TREAT MY CHILDREN
AS THE PEOPLE THEY ARE
AND NOT THE PEOPLE
I WANT THEM TO BE.

I DON'T HAVE TO BE TOLERANT OF MY FAMILY IF THEY CHOOSE TO HARM ME.

I DON'T HAVE TO BE
ACCEPTING OF MY FAMILY IF
THEIR PRESENCE IN MY LIFE
DISRUPTS MY PEACE.

◆

I CHOOSE WHOM I WANT
TO CALL FAMILY. LOVE
TRANSCENDS BIOLOGY.

I RELEASE ALL LINGERING ANGER AND RESENTMENT TOWARD ALL MEMBERS OF MY FAMILY.

I REFUSE TO FORCE A RELATIONSHIP WITH MY FAMILY IF IT DOES ME MORE HARM THAN GOOD.

＊

FIERCE FACT

PATTY JENKINS is a writer and director. Her debut film, *Monster*, a biographical drama about serial killer Aileen Wuornos, earned Charlize Theron the Academy Award for best leading actress in 2004. Despite the critical and commercial success of her first film, Patty struggled to find backers for her projects, and she spent a decade directing TV and commercials. However, in 2015, Patty landed *Wonder Woman*, a superhero film based on the DC Comics starring Gal Gadot in the title role. Released in 2017, *Wonder Woman* earned $228 million in its first weekend, then the biggest opening weekend for a female director ever. It went on to break several more records, including the box office record for highest-grossing film directed by a woman. To direct the *Wonder Woman* sequel, Patty was offered a deal that broke another record: She became the highest-paid female director of all time.

MY GIRLFRIENDS ARE THE
SISTERS I CHOOSE.

◆

I INTERRUPT MY BESTIE
WHEN SHE IS BEING SELF-
DEPRECATING. I WON'T LET
HER TALK TO MY
BEST FRIEND LIKE THAT!

I PRIORITIZE THE QUALITY OF A FRIENDSHIP AND NOT THE LENGTH OF IT.

MY FRIENDS ARE ALWAYS
THERE TO UPLIFT AND
REMIND ME WHO I AM.

◆

I HAVE FRIENDS WHO
SEE THE GREATNESS IN ME
THAT I DO NOT YET SEE.

I DON'T HAVE TO HOLD ON TO FRIENDSHIPS THAT ARE UNHEALTHY FOR MY GROWTH AND SELF-ESTEEM.

I WILL LET GO
OF LONG-HELD RESENTMENT
WITH OLD FRIENDS.
I ACCEPT THAT WE HAVE
ALL GROWN.

◆

I AM LOVED AND RESPECTED
BY MY FRIENDS,
WHOM I LOVE AND RESPECT.

I AM HAPPY TO SEE
MY FRIENDS GROW.
I HAVE NO COMPETITIVE SPIRIT
AGAINST MY FRIENDS.

◆

I CAN MOVE ON FROM
FRIENDS WHO WISH TO BRING
NEGATIVITY INTO MY LIFE.

✳

FIERCE FACT

AUDRE LORDE described herself as a "black, lesbian, mother, warrior, poet." The writer, scholar, and activist was raised in New York City by Grenadian immigrant parents. After obtaining a master's degree in library science, she worked as a librarian for seven years before publishing her first volume of poetry and winning a National Endowment for the Arts grant in 1968, when she was in her mid-30s. Her poetry, novels, and essays critically explored feminism, gender, sexuality, and race. Through her writing and her activism, she challenged oppression and affirmed the dignity of the human spirit.

Audre was openly critical of the lack of intersectionality in feminism. In 1981, she co-founded Kitchen Table: Women of Color Press to support the work of fellow black feminists. Today, Audre Lorde's words still inspire people to be brave and to live authentically. She wrote, "My silences had not protected me. Your silence will not protect you. But for every real word spoken, for every attempt I had ever made to speak those truths for which I am still seeking, I had made contact with other women while we examined the words to fit a world in which we all believed, bridging our differences."

◆

"I DON'T KNOW WHAT
I WOULD HAVE DONE SO MANY
TIMES IN MY LIFE IF I HADN'T
HAD MY GIRLFRIENDS."

REESE WITHERSPOON,
Actor, screenwriter, and producer

CHAPTER 5

◆

105

◆

"WHEN YOU LOVE AND ACCEPT
YOURSELF, WHEN YOU KNOW
WHO REALLY CARES ABOUT YOU,
AND WHEN YOU LEARN FROM
YOUR MISTAKES, THEN YOU STOP
CARING ABOUT WHAT PEOPLE
WHO DON'T KNOW YOU THINK."

BEYONCÉ KNOWLES-CARTER,

Singer, songwriter, producer, and actor

FIERCE FIRST

WILMA MANKILLER

WILMA MANKILLER was born in 1945 on tribal lands in Tahlequah, Oklahoma. As a child, she and her family moved to San Francisco under the Indian Relocation Act. The act was part of a suite of laws and policies known as Indian termination policy, which intended to dismantle tribal sovereignty and Native culture. Her family did not receive the support they needed and struggled in the Bay Area, but they persisted. After high school, Wilma married and had two children.

In 1969, Native college students seized Alcatraz Island, and the year-and-a-half-long protest brought about Wilma's political awakening. She began raising money for these activists, who were fighting for Native rights and demanding the return of many federal lands to Native peoples. Her husband was unsupportive of her burgeoning activism, and so they divorced in 1977.

She returned home to Oklahoma with her daughters and got a bachelor's degree from Flaming Rainbow University.

In 1981, she founded the Cherokee Nation's Community Development Department. She rallied the people of Bell to install a waterline, giving the community running water. "I feel that not just Cherokee people, but poor people in general, have a much greater capacity for leadership and for solving their own problems than they're given credit for," she said.

In 1983, Ross Swimmer, the principal chief of the Cherokee Nation, asked her to run as his deputy principal chief. They won the election. She faced sexist opposition in her leadership role, and at one point when a male tribal elder continuously interrupted her at an important meeting, she simply turned off his microphone. After Ross Swimmer left office in 1985, Wilma took over his seat as principal chief of the Cherokee Nation, becoming the first woman to assume this role. She remained the principal chief after she won her election in 1987. She was reelected with a huge majority of the vote in 1991. Wilma ensured that the Nation was financially solid, and she set up health clinics as well as the Institute for Cherokee Literacy, which worked to preserve Cherokee language and culture.

In 1998, Wilma was awarded the Presidential Medal of Freedom by President Bill Clinton in recognition of her leadership and achievements. She remains an inspiration to women everywhere.

"After leaving even a subconscious fear of death behind, it made me less afraid of life. More courage. It actually enabled me to have the self-confidence and the courage to lead."

—WILMA MANKILLER

MY VALUE LIES IN WHAT
MAKES ME UNIQUE.

◆

I AM IN CONTROL OF WHO
I WANT TO BE.

I WILL GIVE THE WORLD A CHANCE TO EXPERIENCE THE MARVELOUS PERSON I AM.

I WILL TALK TO MYSELF
AS I WOULD TALK TO
SOMEONE I REALLY LOVE.

◆

I AM BRAVE ENOUGH TO
EXPLORE MY GREATNESS.

I WILL NOT BE SHAMED FOR THE PERSON I AM. I AM POWERFUL AND WHOLE.

I AM PROUD OF EXACTLY
WHO I AM, AND I OWE IT
TO MYSELF TO LET MY VOICE
BE HEARD.

◆

FEAR AND DOUBT WILL
NOT DIM MY LIGHTS.
I WAS CREATED TO SHINE.

I WOULD RATHER TELL STORIES OF THE TIMES I TRIED THAN HAVE NOTHING TO SHARE BUT REGRETS.

MY ACTIONS WILL SET THE WORLD ON FIRE. I AM SO BEAUTIFUL WHEN I AM FREE.

FIERCE FACT

After getting her law degree from Harvard and working as an attorney for several years, MICHELLE OBAMA decided she was drawn to public service and started working for the city of Chicago. In 2009, when her husband Barack Obama became the 44th president of the United States, Michelle became the first black First Lady. She used her platform to continue a life of public service.

In 2010, she created Let's Move! to bring attention to the childhood obesity epidemic. Let's Move! worked toward greater access to healthy food and physical activity for children. After the passage of the Healthy, Hunger-Free Kids Act, a law championed by Michelle and Let's Move!, the United States updated its school meal nutritional standards, and 50 million American public school students got access to healthier food.

In 2015, Michelle and Barack Obama teamed up with the Peace Corps, USAID, and the Department of State to launch Let Girls Learn. This initiative helped girls around the world access education.

After leaving the White House, Michelle continued her mission to support girls' education by launching the Girls Opportunity Alliance through the Obama Foundation. This program promotes and steers donations toward the work of grassroots organizations dedicated to educating girls.

MY PAST DOES NOT
DICTATE MY FUTURE.
MY PRESENT IS FILLED
WITH POSSIBILITIES.

◆

I HAVE NO FEAR
OF WHAT PEOPLE SAY
OR THINK ABOUT ME
BECAUSE I LOVE MYSELF.

I DO NOT HAVE TO BE THE PERSON THEY WANT ME TO BE. WHO I AM IS ENOUGH.

I CAN FEEL THE GREATNESS
RADIATING OFF MY SKIN
EVERY SINGLE MOMENT
I CHOOSE MYSELF.

◆

I LOVE THE WOMAN
I AM BECOMING.

I BELIEVE THAT I WILL GET TO WHERE I NEED TO GET TO IN LIFE BECAUSE I AM DETERMINED AND FOCUSED.

I AM MY BEST SELF
WHEN I AM AUTHENTIC
AND TRUE TO MYSELF.

♦

I AM BETTER AT
BEING ME THAN I AM AT
BEING ANYONE ELSE.

I AM CONTENT WITH MY
CURRENT LIFE AND WILL ONLY
SOAR HIGHER AND HIGHER.

◆

I AM LIVING
THE LIFE THAT
IS NECESSARY FOR ME.

FIERCE FACT

CHIMAMANDA NGOZI ADICHIE is an award-winning Nigerian novelist and essayist. A best-selling author, she is globally regarded as an important contemporary voice of African literature. Her novels have been translated into dozens of languages, and in 2008, she won a MacArthur Fellowship—commonly known as the MacArthur Genius Grant—for her fiction writing.

In 2012, she gave the TED Talk "We Should All Be Feminists," which was widely admired by audiences around the world. In the talk, she said, "The problem with gender is that it prescribes how we should be rather than recognizing how we are. Imagine how much happier we would be, how much freer to be our true individual selves, if we didn't have the weight of gender expectations."

In 2014, Chimamanda published a book adapted from her TED Talk. It received overwhelmingly positive reviews globally, and many critics encouraged it as an important read for everyone to learn to embrace life freely without being caged by their gender. The Swedish Women's Lobby bought a copy for every 16-year-old student in the country in 2015.

"FOR ME, BECOMING ISN'T
ABOUT ARRIVING SOMEWHERE
OR ACHIEVING A CERTAIN AIM.
I SEE IT INSTEAD AS FORWARD
MOTION, A MEANS OF EVOLVING,
A WAY TO REACH CONTINUOUSLY
TOWARD A BETTER SELF. THE
JOURNEY DOESN'T END."

MICHELLE OBAMA,

Lawyer, author, and former First Lady of the United States

REFERENCES

"About Us." Nobel Women's Initiative. Accessed February 11, 2020. NobelWomensInitiative.org/about.

Alexander, Kerri Lee. "Janet Mock." National Women's History Museum. Accessed February 11, 2020. WomensHistory.org/education-resources /biographies/janet-mock.

Alexander, Kerri Lee. "Patsy Mink." National Women's History Museum. Accessed February 11, 2020. WomensHistory.org/education-resources /biographies/patsy-mink.

Atherton, Alisa S. "Wilma Mankiller and the Cherokee Nation" (lesson plan, Utah State University, Logan, UT). Accessed February 11, 2020. TeacherLink.ED.USU.edu/tlresources/units/Byrnes-famous/Mankillr.html.

"Audre Lorde." Biography. A&E Networks Television. Updated April 16, 2019. Biography.com/scholar/audre-lorde.

Audre Lorde—The Berlin Years. Accessed February 11, 2020. AudreLorde-TheBerlinYears.com/press_in.html.

Blumberg, Naomi. "Malala Yousafzai." Encyclopædia Britannica. Updated March 11, 2020. Britannica.com/biography/Malala-Yousafzai.

Cartlidge, Cherese. *Beyoncé*. Farmington Hills, MI: Lucent Books, 2012.

Charlie Rose. "Wilma Mankiller." Aired January 12, 1994. CharlieRose.com
/videos/19285.

"Chrissie Wellington." Premiere Speakers Bureau. Accessed February 10,
2020. PremiereSpeakers.com/chrissie-wellington/bio.

Close, Frank. "Vera Rubin Obituary." *The Guardian*. Published January 1,
2017. TheGuardian.com/science/2017/jan/01/vera-rubin-obituary.

"Cross-Cultural Sisterhood: Audre Lorde's Living Legacy in Germany."
The Feminist Wire. Published February 20, 2014. TheFeministWire.com
/2014/02/cross-cultural-sisterhood-audre-lordes-living-legacy-in
-germany-2.

Dahir, Abdi Latif. "Chimamanda Adichie Is Leading the Rise of an African
Literature Wave in China." Quartz Africa. Published January 15, 2019.
QZ.com/africa/1524030/chimamanda-adichie-leads-african-literature
-wave-in-china.

Doak, Robin S. *Dolores Huerta: Labor Leader and Civil Rights Activist*.
Minneapolis: Compass Point Books, 2008.

Dodds, Tracy. "The Indianapolis 500: Why Aren't Women Racing at Indy?
Ask Guthrie." *Los Angeles Times*. Published May 24, 1987.
LATimes.com/archives/la-xpm-1987-05-24-sp-2407-story.html.

"Dolores Huerta." Biography.com. A&E Networks Television. Updated
February 26, 2020. Biography.com/activist/dolores-huerta

Fabrizio, Tony. "Janet Guthrie: Racing's Reluctant Trailblazer Is 'Qualified.'"
ESPN. Published May 27, 2019. ESPN.com/espnw/culture/story/_/id
/26777609/racing-reluctant-trailblazer-qualified.

"Flora Nwapa." Author's Calendar. Accessed February 10, 2020.
AuthorsCalendar.info/nwapa.htm.

Gross, Terry. "Meryl Streep: The Fresh Air Interview." *NPR's Fresh Air*.
Aired February 6, 2012. NPR.org/transcripts/146362798

Hendy, Iheoma. "Who Is Flora Nwapa? The First of Many African
Female Authors." *BuzzNigeria*. Published May 23, 2018.
BuzzNigeria.com/flora-nwapa.

"Interview: In Fighting for Girls' Education, UN Advocate Malala Yousafzai
Finds Her Purpose." UN News, United Nations. Published October 5,
2017. News.UN.org/en/story/2017/10/567872-interview-fighting-girls
-education-un-advocate-malala-yousafzai-finds-her.

Jackson, Jenn M. "Congresswoman Shirley Chisholm's Historic
Presidential Run Was 'Unbought and Unbossed.'" *Teen Vogue*.
February 8, 2019. TeenVogue.com/story/congresswoman-shirley
-chisholm-unbought-and-unbossed.

"Janet Guthrie: A Revolution in Racing." Automotive Hall of Fame.
Published February 6, 2019. AutomotiveHallOfFame.org
/janet-guthrie-a-revolution-in-racing.

Kettler, Sara. "Malala Yousafzai." Biography.com. A&E Networks Television. Updated February 19, 2019. Biography.com/activist/malala-yousafzai.

Kwon, RO "Your Silence Will Not Protect You by Audre Lorde Review—Prophetic and Necessary." *The Guardian*. Published October 4, 2017. TheGuardian.com/books/2017/oct/04/your-silence-will-not-protect-you-by-audre-lorder-review.

Larsen, Kristine. "Vera Cooper Rubin." Jewish Women's Archive. Accessed February 11, 2020. JWA.org/encyclopedia/article/rubin-vera-cooper.

"Learn More about Shirley Chisholm." Brooklyn College. Accessed February 11, 2020. Brooklyn.CUNY.edu/web/academics/schools/socialsciences/interdisciplinary/undergraduate/womens/chisholmproject/learn_more.php.

Levine, Nick. "The Guide to Getting Into Madonna, Holy Mother of Modern Pop." Vice. Published June 13, 2019. Vice.com/en_ca/article/8xzeg4/how-to-get-into-madonna-best-music.

Maathai, Wangari. *Unbowed: A Memoir*. New York: Anchor Books, 2006.

Marchese, David. "In Conversation: Chimamanda Ngozi Adichie." *Vulture*. Published July 9, 2018. Vulture.com/2018/07/chimamanda-ngozi-adichie-in-conversation.html.

Martinelli, Michelle R. "Racing Trailblazer Janet Guthrie Reflects on Indy 500 and Sexism in Motor Sports." *USA Today*. Published May 26, 2019. FTW.USAToday.com/2019/05/indy-500-janet-guthrie-sexism-nascar -motor-sports-espn-qualified.

McIntyre, Gina. "'Wonder Woman' Director Patty Jenkins: 'We Need a New Kind of Hero.'" *Rolling Stone*. Published June 2, 2017. RollingStone.com/movies/movie-features/wonder-woman-director -patty-jenkins-we-need-a-new-kind-of-hero-193705.

Michals, Debra. "Dolores Huerta." National Women's History Museum. Accessed February 10, 2020. WomensHistory.org/education-resources /biographies/dolores-huerta.

Michals, Debra. "Shirley Chisholm." National Women's History Museum. Accessed February 11, 2020. WomensHistory.org /education-resources/biographies/shirley-chisholm.

"Mink, Patsy Takemoto." US House of Representatives: History, Art & Archives. Accessed February 11, 2020. History.House.gov/People /detail/18329.

"Mrs. Saroljini Naidu." Indian National Congress. Accessed February 20, 2020. Inc.in/en/leadership/past-party-president/mrs-sarojini-naidu.

Nessif, Bruna. "Reese Witherspoon Talks Success, Girlfriends' Support and Baby Tennessee Stealing Her Brain in *Red Magazine*." *E! News*. Published April 29, 2013. EOnline.com/fr/news/412641/reese-witherspoon-talks-success-girlfriends-support-and-baby-tennessee-stealing-her-brain-in-red-magazine.

Obama, Michelle. *Becoming*. New York: Crown, 2018.

"Once a Physicist: Janet Guthrie." Institute of Physics. Accessed February 10, 2020. IOP.org/careers/working-life/profiles/page_60280.html#gref.

"Our History." The Green Belt Movement. Accessed February 11, 2020. GreenBeltMovement.org/who-we-are/our-history.

Overbye, Dennis. "Vera Rubin, 88, Dies; Opened Doors in Astronomy, and for Women." *New York Times*. Published December 27, 2016.

"Patsy Takemoto Mink." National Women's Hall of Fame. Accessed February 11, 2020. WomenOfTheHall.org/inductee/patsy-takemoto-mink.

"Patty Jenkins." IMDb. Accessed February 11, 2020. IMDb.com/name/nm0420941.

Petersen, Carolyn Collins. "The Life and Times of Dr. Vera Cooper Rubin: Astronomy Pioneer." *ThoughtCo*. Published December 5, 2018. ThoughtCo.com/vera-cooper-rubin-biography-4120939.

Ramos, Dorkys. "Jada Pinkett Smith: Raise Our Daughters to Be the Women They Want to Be." BET. Published May 10, 2013. BET.com /news/lifestyle/2013/05/10/jada-pinkett-smith-raise-our-daughters-to -be-the-women-they-want-to-be.html.

Rhimes, Shonda. *Year of Yes: How to Dance It Out, Stand In the Sun, and Be Your Own Person*. New York: Simon & Schuster, 2015.

Schnall, Marianne. "Interview with Wangari Maathai." Accessed February 11, 2020. Feminist.com/resources/artspeech/interviews /wangarimaathai.html.

"Shirley Chisholm." History, A&E Television Networks. December 18, 2009. History.com/topics/us-politics/shirley-chisholm.

"Shonda Rhimes." Biography.com. A&E Networks Television. Updated August 27, 2019. Biography.com/media-figure/shonda-rhimes.

Stephenson, Kristen. "2019: A Record-Breaking Year for Simone Biles." Guinness World Records. Published December 18, 2019. GuinnessWorldRecords.com/news/2019/12/2019-a-record-breaking -year-for-simone-biles-603292.

Strehlke, Sade. "How August Cover Star Simone Biles Blazes Through Expectations." *Teen Vogue*. Published June 30, 2016. TeenVogue.com /story/simone-biles-summer-olympics-cover-august-2016.

Sullivan, Patricia. "Modern Cherokees' First Female Chief, Wilma
Mankiller, Excelled over Hardship." *The Washington Post*. Published
April 7, 2010. WashingtonPost.com/wp-dyn/content/article/2010/04/06
/AR2010040603469.html.

TED. "Chimamanda Ngozi Adichie." Accessed February 11, 2020. Ted.com
/speakers/chimamanda_ngozi_adichie.

Tyler, Ray. "Wilma Mankiller." National Women's History Museum. Accessed
February 11, 2020. WomensHistory.org/education-resources/biographies
/wilma-mankiller

Ulysse, Gina Athena. "How Audre Lorde Made Queer History." *Ms.
Magazine*. Published October 31, 2011. MsMagazine.com/2011/10/31
/how-audre-lorde-made-queer-history.

VanZenten, Susan. "A Conversation with Chimamanda Ngozi Adichie."
Image Journal. Accessed February 11, 2020. ImageJournal.org/article
/conversation-chimamanda-ngozi-adichie.

"Wangari Maathai." The Green Belt Movement. Accessed February 11,
2020. GreenBeltMovement.org/wangari-maathai/biography.

Wellington, Chrissie. "Ironman Champ: Your Mind Matters More." CNN.
Published July 13, 2012. CNN.com/2012/07/13/health/mind-over-matter
-wellington/index.html.

Williams, Vanessa. "'Unbought and Unbossed': Shirley Chisholm's Feminist Mantra Is Still Relevant 50 Years Later." *Washington Post*. Published January 26, 2018. WashingtonPost.com/news/post-nation/wp/2018/01/26/unbought-and-unbossed-shirley-chisholms-feminist-mantra-is-as-relevant-today-as-it-was-50-years-ago.

Winfrey, Oprah. "What Oprah Knows for Sure about Finding the Courage to Follow Your Dreams." Accessed February 20, 2020. Oprah.com/spirit/what-oprah-knows-for-sure-about-finding-your-dreams.

Yousafzai, Malala. "Nobel Lecture." December 10, 2014. Oslo, Norway. NobelPrize.org/prizes/peace/2014/yousafzai/26074-malala-yousafzai-nobel-lecture-2014.

Yiu, Yuen. "Remembering Vera Rubin." Inside Science. Published December 28, 2016. InsideScience.org/news/remembering-vera-rubin.

Zwerin, Michael. "The Real Nina Simone." In *DownBeat: The Great Jazz Interviews: A 75th Anniversary Anthology*, edited by Frank Alkyer and Ed Enright. Milwaukee, WI: Hal Leonard Books, 2009.

INDEX